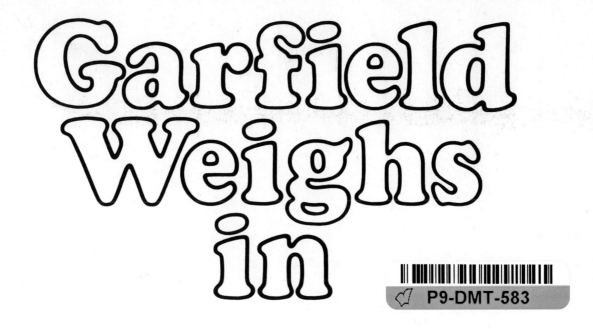

Garfield Weighs in

BY: JIM DAVIS

BALLANTINE BOOKS · NEW YORK

All rights reserved under International and Pan-American Copyright
Conventions. Published in the United States by Ballantine Books,
a division of Random House, Inc., New York, and simultaneously
in Canada by Random House of Canada Limited, Toronto, Canada.

Library of Congress Catalog Card Number: 81-69192
ISBN 0-345-30262-1

Manufactured in the United States of America

First Ballantine Books Edition: March 1982

1 2 3 4 5 6 7 8 9 10

BONK!

GARFIELD HATES MONDAYS

I HATE MONDAYS

JIM DAVIS © 1980 United Feature Syndicate, Inc.

4-7

4-8

YOU'RE GREAT, GARFIELD

© 1980 United Feature Syndicate, Inc.

YOU'RE WARM, FURRY, CUDDLY, AND...

IF YOU SAY "CUTE" I'LL SCRATCH YOUR EYES OUT

JIM DAVIS

THIS IS GREAT. I HAVE A DATE WITH LIZ. I'LL FINALLY HAVE HER ALL TO MYSELF

JUST HER AND ME

AND KITTY MAKES THREE

4-23   JIM DAVIS

WHAT DO YOU HAVE PLANNED FOR US TONIGHT?

4-24

FIRST WE'LL JET TO A HOLLYWOOD PREMIERE AND RECEPTION WITH THE STARS. THEN HAVE AN INTIMATE DINNER AT A POSH RESTAURANT FOLLOWED BY AN EVENING OF DANCING AT A PRIVATE CLUB TOPPED OFF WITH BUBBLY ON THE BEACH AT SUNRISE

YOU'RE KIDDING!

YES...HOW DOES A DRIVE-IN MOVIE GRAB YOU?

YEA

© 1980 United Feature Syndicate, Inc.   JIM DAVIS

© 1980 United Feature Syndicate, Inc.

EAT UP, PAL

JIM DAVIS

5-2

I WON'T SAY GARFIELD IS FAT, BUT THE LAST TIME HE GOT ON A FERRIS WHEEL, THE TWO GUYS ON TOP STARVED TO DEATH

SPLAT!

© 1980 United Feature Syndicate, Inc.

5-3

I MUST SPEAK TO JON ABOUT CHANGING THE WATER IN MY BOWL

JIM DAVIS

WHAT'S HAPPENING?

I HAVE NO URGE TO SHOVE ODIE OFF THE TABLE!

5-4

I'M LOSING MY TOUCH!

I MUST BE HAVING AN ATTACK OF NICE!

© 1980 United Feature Syndicate, Inc.

PUSH

WITH SELF-CONTROL YOU CAN CONQUER ANYTHING

JIM DAVIS

5-12

JIM DAVIS

NOW WHERE COULD MY RUBBER MOUSIE BE?

5-13

EIYEEEEE!

SPLASH!

THAT'S RIGHT. I LEFT IT IN THE BATHTUB

JIM DAVIS

GARFIELD! WHY WOULD YOU EVER WANT TO CATCH THAT FISH?

© 1980 United Feature Syndicate, Inc.   5-16

SOME PEOPLE **LOVE** CATS FOR WHAT THEY **ARE**...

AND SOME PEOPLE **ARE** CATS FOR WHAT THEY **LOVE**

JIM DAVIS

© 1980 United Feature Syndicate, Inc.   5-17

WHAT'S THE MATTER, JON? CAT GOT YOUR TONGUE?

YOU MIGHT THAY THAT

JIM DAVIS

5-19

JIM DAVIS © 1980 United Feature Syndicate, Inc.

MY PIANO'S POSSESSED!
THERE'S AN EVIL SPIRIT
IN MY PIANO!

5-20

YOU TAKE
THAT BACK!

JIM DAVIS

© 1980 United Feature Syndicate, Inc.

GOOD DAY, SPORTS FREAKS. WELCOME TO YOUR FIRST TENNIS LESSON

5-21

FIRST, HOLD YOUR TENNIS RACQUET JUST LIKE THIS...

NOW DRAIN YOUR SPAGHETTI WITH IT

© 1980 United Feature Syndicate, Inc. JIM DAVIS

GASP. STRUGGLE WHEEZE

5-22

LASAGNA! I NEED LASAGNA!

LET'S TALK ABOUT THIS PASTA DEPENDENCY OF YOURS, GARFIELD

FIRST, A NOODLE, THEN WE TALK

JIM DAVIS © 1980 United Feature Syndicate, Inc.

I'LL JUST TAKE THE LAST HELPING OF LASAGNA, GARFIELD

5-23 © 1980 United Feature Syndicate, Inc.

AND YOU MAY DO WHATEVER YOU WISH WITH THE PAN, HA-HA

WHANG!

SPLAT!

JIM DAVIS

I'M GETTING TIRED OF YOUR STRONG-ARM TACTICS AROUND HERE, GARFIELD

5-24

REMEMBER: BLESSED ARE THE MEEK: FOR THEY SHALL INHERIT THE EARTH

BUT, IN THE MEANTIME, THE STRONG WILL MAKE A PRETTY COMFORTABLE LIVING

© 1980 United Feature Syndicate, Inc.   JIM DAVIS

GRAB!

STRETCH

PTING!

KABOING!

ZOOM!

FLAP
FLAP
FLAP

THAT'S THE DARNDEST
THING I'VE EVER SEEN

JIM
DAVIS

5-25

© 1980 United Feature Syndicate, Inc.

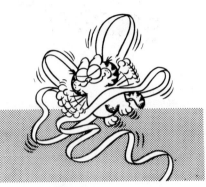

5-28

SPLOOT!

WHAT'S THAT?

LEMON MERINGUE ODIE

JIM DAVIS © 1980 United Feature Syndicate, Inc.

♪ HERE, ODIE!

5-29 © 1980 United Feature Syndicate, Inc.

I'M GOING TO TRAIN YOU TO SIT UP TODAY

IT'S HARD TO TEACH A DEAD DOG NEW TRICKS

JIM DAVIS

SOME PEOPLE SAY I'M MEAN TO ODIE. DON'T GET ME WRONG, I **LOVE** DOGS. AND IF I'M LYING, MAY LIGHTNING ...

5-30 © 1980 United Feature Syndicate, Inc.

STRIKE THE DOG NEXT DOOR

KERPOW!
YIP!

JIM DAVIS

TO PROPERLY ENJOY TENNIS YOU MUST HAVE THE CORRECT STANCE

5-31

YOU'LL HAVE TO IMAGINE THE EASY CHAIR, TV, AND SIX-PACK

JIM DAVIS © 1980 United Feature Syndicate, Inc.

TIME TO PUT YOU OUT, GARFIELD

I DON'T WANNA GO OUT!

© 1980 United Feature Syndicate, Inc.

SLAM!

6-1

JIM DAVIS

SLURP!

YUK

LOOK, ODIE... ME CAT, YOU DOG, WE FIGHT. THAT'S THE ORDER OF THINGS

6-8

UNDERSTAND?

SLURP!

© 1980 United Feature Syndicate, Inc.

JIM DAVIS

THE JUNGLE CAT AWAKES WITH A VORACIOUS APPETITE

© 1980 United Feature Syndicate, Inc.

6-9

HE INSTINCTIVELY SETS OUT TO SLAY SOME BREAKFAST

GARFIELD

THAT WASN'T VERY PRETTY, BUT IT'S ALL PART OF THE FOOD CHAIN

JIM DAVIS

GARFIELD

THE ALLEY CAT SCROUNGES FOR FOOD

6-10

HE POKES HIS HEAD INTO A PROMISING GARBAGE CAN

PEEEYEWWW!

© 1980 United Feature Syndicate, Inc.

JIM DAVIS

THE ACTOR CAT IS BEING FILMED ESCAPING FROM THE ENEMY

6-13 © 1980 United Feature Syndicate, Inc.

HE MUST LEAP OFF A CLIFF TO COMPLETE THE ESCAPE

WHICH, OF COURSE, IS DONE BY A STUNT DOG

JIM DAVIS

THE HOUSE CAT HAS A BUSY SCHEDULE

© 1980 United Feature Syndicate, Inc. 6-14

WHAT WITH SHARPENING CLAWS

AND SEEING HIS OWNER OFF ON A BIG NIGHT

JIM DAVIS

TOMORROW I'LL BE TWO YEARS OF AGE. THAT'S THE HUMAN EQUIVALENT OF FOURTEEN

6-18

CATS HAVE IT GOOD

ADOLESCENCE WITHOUT ACNE

JIM DAVIS © 1980 United Feature Syndicate, Inc.

TODAY IS MY BIRTHDAY, AND I HATE BIRTHDAYS. I'M GOING TO GET A SURPRISE PARTY, AND I HATE SURPRISE PARTIES

JIM DAVIS © 1980 United Feature Syndicate, Inc.

SURPRISE, GARFIELD!

BUT I LOOOOOVE THE ATTENTION!

6-19

6-22

JiM DAViS

© 1980 United Feature Syndicate, Inc.

WHEW. I CAN'T FINISH MY MEAL

6-23

WHAT AM I SAYING?!!

IT JUST WOULDN'T BE GARFIELD TO LEAVE FOOD

© 1980 United Feature Syndicate, Inc. JIM DAVIS

JIM DAVIS © 1980 United Feature Syndicate, Inc.

WHUMP!

6-24

DARN.
I CAN'T
SLEEP

SLUP

MILK

PUFF
PUFF

© 1980 United Feature Syndicate, Inc.   6-29

JIM DAVIS

OH NO! HERE COMES THE SLUDGE MONSTER!

7-4

© 1980 United Feature Syndicate, Inc.

ARRGH!

I WISH YOU'D CURB THAT IMAGINATION OF YOURS, GARFIELD

JIM DAVIS

THERE IT IS!

© 1980 United Feature Syndicate, Inc.

7-5

PREPARE TO MEET YOUR MAKER, SLUDGE MONSTER!

WHY DID YOU MANGLE THAT LIVER, GARFIELD?

IN THE INTEREST OF NATIONAL SECURITY, SIR

JIM DAVIS

IT'S MONDAY, GARFIELD. WHAT ARE YOU GOING TO DO TODAY?

7-7

WHAT EVERYONE SHOULD DO ON MONDAY

SLEEP TILL TUESDAY

JIM DAVIS © 1980 United Feature Syndicate, Inc.

SO THIS IS TUESDAY

7-8

DO YOU KNOW WHAT I LIKE MOST ABOUT TUESDAY?

IT'S NOT MONDAY

JIM DAVIS © 1980 United Feature Syndicate, Inc.

SLURP!

SLURP!

I THINK I STRAINED SOMETHING

7-11 © 1980 United Feature Syndicate, Inc.

JIM DAVIS

RING!

7-12

SMACK!

A LITTLE HIGH-STRUNG AREN'T WE?

I'M A CAT. SO SUE ME

JIM DAVIS © 1980 United Feature Syndicate, Inc.

WHAT A BEAUTIFUL DAY!

SNIFF

© 1980 United Feature Syndicate, Inc.

STING!

KONK!

7-13

JiM DAViS

BONK!

CLONK!

WHAT THE...?

IT'S NOT NICE TO FOOL WITH MOTHER NATURE

IT'S ANOTHER BRAND NEW DAY FOR GARFIELD, THE BIGGEST, BADDEST, MEANEST CAT IN THE LAND

7-16

AND HIS SIDEKICK, POOKY

THE BIGGEST, BADDEST, MEANEST TEDDY BEAR

JIM DAVIS © 1980 United Feature Syndicate, Inc.

7-17

© 1980 United Feature Syndicate, Inc. JIM DAVIS

7-18

POOKY! SPEAK TO ME! ARE YOU OKAY, FELLA?

© 1980 United Feature Syndicate, Inc. JIM DAVIS

HEY, BOBBI BABY! WHAT'S HAPPENIN'?

7-19

YOU SAY I GOT A WRONG NUMBER? WELL FOR A WRONG NUMBER YOU SURE HAVE A SEXY VOICE. WHO IS THIS?

JIM DAVIS

OH, HI, MOM

EMBARRASSMENT CITY

© 1980 United Feature Syndicate, Inc.

OKAY, ATTACK CAT, LET'S SAY A MUGGER JUMPS OUT OF THE BUSHES

7-25

A 300-POUND MUGGER WITH A CLUB

HOW WILL WE EVER PROTECT OURSELVES?

HE'S NOT AFTER **MY** WALLET, JACK

JIM DAVIS

FORGET IT, GARFIELD. YOU'LL NEVER MAKE A GOOD ATTACK CAT

7-26

OH YEH? WELL JUST LET SOME BRUTE TRY TO MUG JON

I'LL GIVE HIM THE HISSING OF HIS LIFE

JIM DAVIS

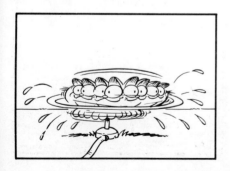

HOP   HOP

THAT'S THE THING ABOUT CANNED SALMON

HOP

IT'S EASIER TO CATCH WHEN IT HEADS UPSTREAM TO SPAWN

8-1

JIM DAVIS

GRRRR

© 1980 United Feature Syndicate, Inc.

8-2

ROWR!

ONE OF THESE DAYS THIS FIERCE ROUTINE'S GONNA GET ME CREAMED

YIP YIP YIP

JIM DAVIS

© 1980 United Feature Syndicate, Inc.

JIM DAVIS

8-3

YOU'LL HAVE TO ADMIT, GARFIELD...

8-8

NOW THAT YOU'RE ON A DIET, YOU'RE FEELING BETTER ABOUT YOURSELF

YOU BET

ASIDE FROM THE HUNGER, DIZZINESS AND WEAKNESS, I'M HAVING A BALL

JIM DAVIS © 1980 United Feature Syndicate, Inc.

YOU'RE THE CORRECT WEIGHT...

8-9 © 1980 United Feature Syndicate, Inc.

FOR AN AIRCRAFT CARRIER, HA-HA

I SHOULDN'T HAVE SAID THAT

JIM DAVIS

DON'T LIKE YOUR CAT FOOD, HUH?

8-15

IS THERE ANYTHING I CAN GIVE IT?

LAST RITES COMES TO MIND

© 1980 United Feature Syndicate, Inc. JIM DAVIS

YOU'VE FINALLY DONE IT, GARFIELD

8-16   © 1980 United Feature Syndicate, Inc.

YOU'VE TANGLED WITH SOMETHING BIGGER THAN YOU

YEH, BUT YOU SHOULD SEE THE OTHER TRUCK

JIM DAVIS

HEY, GARFIELD, WE'RE GOING TO VISIT DAD AND MOM ON THE FARM THIS WEEK

© 1980 United Feature Syndicate, Inc.

WHERE ARE YOU GOING?

TO PACK MY BIBS, AND STUFF SOME HAYSEEDS BETWEEN MY TEETH

8-18

JIM DAVIS

SAY, MOM, WHATEVER HAPPENED TO NADINE, MY PET CHICKEN?

SHE'S FINE

JIM DAVIS

THIS IS GREAT! WHAT IS IT?

NADINE NOODLE SOUP

SHE WAS FAMILY!

8-19

© 1980 United Feature Syndicate, Inc.

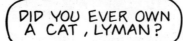

GARFIELD, THERE'S NOTHING YOU CAN DO OR SAY TO MAKE ME SHARE MY LASAGNA WITH YOU

9-27

NOW THAT WAS AN EFFECTIVE LITTLE PLOY

JIM DAVIS © 1980 United Feature Syndicate, Inc.

© 1980 United Feature Syndicate, Inc.   JIM DAVIS

FLIP

9-28

FLIP!

YOU'RE A LOUSY READER, GARFIELD

YOU PLAY A LOUSY GAME OF FLIP, FELLA

SCRATCH
SCRATCH
SCRATCH
SCRATCH
SCRATCH

© 1980 United Feature Syndicate, Inc.

JIM DAVIS

WOOF
WOOF

8-30

RRRRRR

© 1980 United Feature Syndicate, Inc.

EEK, EEK, SHIVER
WITH FRIGHT, BEG FOR
MERCY, RACE UP A TREE

JIM DAVIS

JiM DAViS

B-31

HOW IS IT YOU CATS KNOW EXACTLY WHEN TO BE UNDERFOOT?

LUCKY I GUESS

GARFIELD'S HISTORY OF DOGS

THE WORLD'S FIRST DOG CRAWLED OUT OF THE SEA ABOUT TEN MILLION YEARS AGO

9-1

BUT, UNFORTUNATELY FOR HIM...

© 1980 United Feature Syndicate, Inc.

HE WAS IMMEDIATELY NABBED BY THE WORLD'S FIRST DOGCATCHER

JIM DAVIS

GARFIELD'S HISTORY OF DOGS

TAIL WAGGING WAS INVENTED BY A DOG NAMED "BONZO WAG"

HE FOUND TAIL WAGGING ENDEARED HIM TO HUMANS

© 1980 United Feature Syndicate, Inc.

BONZO ALSO INVENTED SLOBBERING, BUT THAT DIDN'T GO OVER SO WELL

9-2

JIM DAVIS

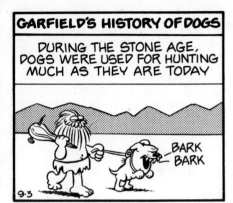

GARFIELD'S HISTORY OF DOGS

DURING THE STONE AGE, DOGS WERE USED FOR HUNTING MUCH AS THEY ARE TODAY

BARK BARK

9-3

GRRRR

© 1980 United Feature Syndicate, Inc.

TIMES WERE TOUGH THEN

STOMP!

JIM DAVIS

GARFIELD'S HISTORY OF DOGS

CONTRARY TO POPULAR BELIEF...

9-4

THE FIRST DOGS WERE **HAPPY** TO MEET THE FIRST CAT

FOR, UNTIL THEN, ALL THEY HAD TO CHASE UP TREES WERE ROCKS

ARF

© 1980 United Feature Syndicate, Inc.

JIM DAVIS

GARFIELD'S HISTORY OF DOGS

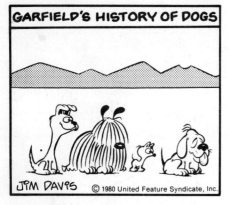

JIM DAVIS © 1980 United Feature Syndicate, Inc.

THE FIRST FIRE HYDRANT

9-5

DOGS' HISTORIC ROLES
AS HUNTERS, PROTECTORS,
TRACKERS, LABORERS
AND COMPANIONS HAVE
CULMINATED TO MAKE MODERN
DOG WHAT HE IS TODAY

JIM DAVIS © 1980 United Feature Syndicate, Inc.

IT COULD
JUST MAKE
YOU CRY

9-6

DO YOU FEEL PERSONALLY RESPONSIBLE FOR THE WORLD FOOD SHORTAGE?

EVERY TIME YOU GO TO THE BEACH, DOES THE TIDE COME IN?

HAVE YOU EVER EATEN AN ENTIRE MOOSE?

CAN YOU SEE YOUR NECK?

DO JOGGERS TAKE LAPS AROUND YOU FOR EXERCISE?

IF SO, WELCOME TO **NATIONAL FAT WEEK!**

JIM DAVIS

9-7

THIS WEEK WE'LL EAT WITHOUT GUILT, AND KICK OFF OUR MEMBERSHIP CAMPAIGN...

BY FORCE-FEEDING A BOX OF CORNSTARCH TO A SKINNY PERSON

HERE'S A NATIONAL FAT WEEK HANDY FACT...

9-10

60% OF THE PEOPLE IN OUR NATION ARE INVOLVED IN SOME WAY WITH THE FOOD INDUSTRY

THAT'S RIGHT. EATING IS NOT ONLY FUN, IT'S PATRIOTIC!

© 1980 United Feature Syndicate, Inc.   JIM DAVIS

THIS YEAR, LET'S CELEBRATE NATIONAL FAT WEEK BY STAMPING OUT FAT JOKES

9-11

LET'S FACE IT, FATTIES...

WE SHOULD BE ABLE TO STAMP OUT ANYTHING WE WISH

© 1980 United Feature Syndicate, Inc.   JIM DAVIS

WE FAT PEOPLE ARE CONSTANTLY BEING DISCRIMINATED AGAINST

AIRPLANE AND THEATER SEATS ARE TOO SMALL. DESIGNER CLOTHING IS NOT MADE IN OUR SIZE. BUT THAT'S TRIVIAL.

9-12

WHAT THIS WORLD REALLY NEEDS IS A KING-SIZE SANDBOX

JIM DAVIS © 1980 United Feature Syndicate, Inc.

HERE'S A NATIONAL FAT WEEK DIET JOKE:

9-13

WHAT WOULD YOU GET IF YOU CROSS A DIETER WITH A NINE-FOOT GORILLA?

YOU GET A GORILLA WHO DIETS ANYWHERE HE PLEASES

© 1980 United Feature Syndicate, Inc. JIM DAVIS

OH, GARFIEEELD ♪

GO FETCH THE PAPER

YOU GOTTA BE KIDDING

NO PAPER, NO BREAKFAST

THAT'S BLACKMAIL

GOOD BOY!

© 1980 United Feature Syndicate, Inc.

9-14

JIM DAVIS

9-15

© 1980 United Feature Syndicate, Inc.

HUNGRY, GARFIELD?

BINGO

JIM DAVIS

9-16

UH-OH, HERE COMES JON!

© 1980 United Feature Syndicate, Inc.

JIM DAVIS

GARFIELD

9-22
JIM DAVIS

WILL YOU GET OUT OF MY FLOWER BOX AND COME TO LUNCH?

GARFIELD
© 1980 United Feature Syndicate, Inc.

NO THANKS. I JUST ATE

I WON'T SAY YOU'RE FAT, GARFIELD...

9-23
JIM DAVIS

BUT I WILL SAY YOU'RE TWO OF THE FINEST CATS I'VE EVER HAD

LET'S SEE... HAIRDRESSERS, HEARING AIDS, HIT MEN

PHONE BOOK

© 1980 United Feature Syndicate, Inc.

SPLOT!

© 1980 United Feature Syndicate, Inc.

LET ME GUESS. YOU'RE TRYING TO TELL ME YOU DON'T LIKE YOUR MEAL

IN MY OWN SUBTLE WAY

WE CATS ARE VERY UNIQUE

WHO ELSE HAS OUR PRIDE, STYLE AND SOPHISTICATION?

© 1980 United Feature Syndicate, Inc.

WHO ELSE CAN KILL AN AFTERNOON HANGING ON THE SCREEN DOOR?

9-26

SLAM!

© 1980 United Feature Syndicate, Inc.   JIM DAVIS

9-27   JIM DAVIS

GOBBLE!
GOBBLE!
GOBBLE!

© 1980 United Feature Syndicate, Inc.

THANKS FOR LEAVING A WING, GARFIELD

WHAT ARE FRIENDS FOR?

THIS CHAIR COULD USE SOME SOFTENING UP

BOING BOING BOING

9-28

JIM DAVIS

SCRATCH SCRATCH SCRATCH

MUCH BETTER

© 1980 United Feature Syndicate, Inc.

SPROING

JUST WHEN A CHAIR EARNS YOUR RESPECT, IT TURNS ON YOU

HMMM, JON'S GOLF CAP

NO ONE DRIVES FASTER THAN THE GREAT ENZIO BODONI

ALMS FOR A TAP DANCING CAT

TAPPITY TAPPITY

CHECK THAT OIL, MISTER?

QUACK QUACK QUACK

10-5

SOMETIMES I WORRY ABOUT YOU, GARFIELD

HA HA HA HA

JIM DAVIS

WHAT ARE YOU DOING UP THERE, GARFIELD?

COME A LITTLE CLOSER AND ASK THAT AGAIN

I'LL GET YOU OUT, GARFIELD

CLUNK!

GEE, IS THERE ANYTHING I CAN DO FOR YOU?

NOTIFY YOUR NEXT OF KIN

KICK!

© 1980 United Feature Syndicate, Inc.

WHERE DID NERMAL GO?

HE'S TAKING A SHORT NAP

CLOP CLOP

HA HA, CATS ARE SO CUTE WHEN THEY PLAY DRESS-UP

© 1980 United Feature Syndicate, Inc.

CUTE TO A POINT, THAT IS

SCRATCH
SCRATCH
SCRATCH

GARFIELD, WHAT WOULD YOU SAY IF I SAID MY CHAIR IS DAMAGED?

I'D SAY YOU'RE RIGHT

WHAT WOULD YOU SAY IF I SAID THE DAMAGE LOOKS LIKE IT WAS DONE BY A CAT?

I'D SAY THERE DO APPEAR TO BE SOME ABRASIONS OF THE CLAW PERSUASION

© 1980 United Feature Syndicate, Inc.

WHAT WOULD YOU SAY IF I SAID WE BOTH KNOW THIS CAT?

I'D SAY YOU'RE GETTING WARM

WHAT WOULD YOU SAY IF I SAID YOU ARE THE CAT WHO SCRATCHED MY CHAIR?

I'D SAY THAT IS A DISTINCT POSSIBILITY

10-19

WHAT WOULD YOU SAY IF I SAID NEVER SHARPEN YOUR CLAWS ON MY CHAIR AGAIN?

NO COMPRENDO, SEÑOR

JIM DAVIS

SCRATCH
SCRATCH
SCRATCH
SCRATCH

10-20

SCRATCH
SCRATCH
SCRATCH
SCRATCH

JIM DAVIS

ME, GARFIELD THE CAT,
A WALKING FLEA CIRCUS.
WHAT A BUMMER

I DON'T MIND
THE ITCHING
OR BITING

BUT THE LIGHTS
FROM THE MIDWAY
ARE KEEPING
ME AWAKE

10-21

JIM DAVIS

BATH TIME!

JIM DAVIS

SPLASH!

© 1980 United Feature Syndicate, Inc.

CLOSE, BUT
NO BANANA

10-26

10-31

11-1

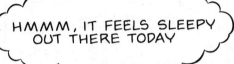

© 1980 United Feature Syndicate, Inc.   11-2

JIM DAVIS

About Jim Davis, creator of GARFIELD

Jim Davis was born July 28, 1945, in Marion, Indiana. After growing up on a farm near Fairmount, Indiana, with about 25 cats, Jim attended Ball State University in Muncie. As an Art and Business major he distinguished himself by earning one of the lowest accumulative grade point averages in the history of the university.

During a two-year stint at a local advertising agency Jim met and married wife, Carolyn, a gifted singer and elementary school teacher.

In 1969 he became the assistant to Tom Ryan on the syndicated comic strip, TUMBLEWEEDS. In addition to cartooning, Jim maintained a career as a freelance commercial artist, copywriter, and radio-talent and political-campaign promoter.

His hobbies include chess, sandwiches, and good friends. A new pastime is playing with his two-year-old son, James Alexander.

In 1978 United Feature Syndicate gave the nod to GARFIELD.

Jim explains, "GARFIELD is strictly an entertainment strip built around the strong personality of a fat, lazy, cynical cat. It's the funniest strip I've ever seen. GARFIELD consciously avoids any social or political comment. My grasp of the world situation isn't that firm anyway. For years, I thought OPEC was a denture adhesive."

The strip is pumped out daily, in a cheerful atmosphere among friends. Valette Hildebrand is assistant cartoonist, Brian Strater is art director for merchandising, Neil Altekruse is production director, Jill Hahn is office manager, and Julie Hamilton is president of Paws, Incorporated, the company that handles the merchandising of the characters in the strip.

"To what do I attribute my cartooning ability?" Jim asks. "As a child I was asthmatic. I was stuck indoors with little more than my imagination and paper and pencil to play with. While asthma worked for me, I wouldn't recommend it for everyone.

"Do I like cartooning?...It's nice work if you can get it."